Reservations on a Cloud

Reservations on a Cloud

Joe Harris

authorHOUSE®

AuthorHouse™
1663 Liberty Drive
Bloomington, IN 47403
www.authorhouse.com
Phone: 1-800-839-8640

First published by AuthorHouse   05/03/2011

ISBN: 978-1-4634-0289-1 (sc)
ISBN: 978-1-4634-0290-7 (ebk)

Library of Congress Control Number: 2011907134

Printed in the United States of America

Any people depicted in stock imagery provided by Thinkstock are models, and such images are being used for illustrative purposes only.
Certain stock imagery © Thinkstock.

This book is printed on acid-free paper.

Dedicated
To
Roslyn Rose and Jeana Rouse, who've been blessings in my life. Enlightened
spirits, architects of hope.

Contents

ACT I

The mind's tongue

Small World

Wings of butterflies . . .
Life's beauty is often compressed
by the speed at which it passes.
Our freedom underlies
imprisoned aspirations; we're caressed
by vengeance, burned by its ashes.
Made in God's image, yet still unperfected
we're all connected,
worlds apart though we intersect.
Engaging ambivalence, sad to see,
hard to change in retrospect
even with a strong plea.
The truth blemished by knaves.
The world's demise predicted before it transpires.
From time to time the thing our life craves
helps more than that which it acquires.

Resistance

Like a ship battered at sea,
so are our lives as we try to find the wheel
to navigate homeostasis.
Perseverance is key
to survive such an ordeal.
Adaptability is rooted in the basis
of our existence.
The will within resistance.
See a reflection tainted by a ripping tide.
Humility drowned in a wave of pride.
Fools of greed, sloth
blinded in their course by a cloth
of gluttony and excess . . .
Couldn't let go of wrath,
collapsing down a bread crumb path.
Grasping desires, baneful to express.
In distress we speed without brakes,
dim the light; hence our mistakes
in the dark are magnified.
Are we ever truly satisfied?
Pirates for these earthly treasures,
risking our soul for these fleshly pleasures.
But far is the length of desperate measures,
paddling the waters of conformity
with oars of individuality

ShatterStar

I lay in admiration
of an affable moon,
reviving our conversations
until sleep welcomes me to my dreams doors.
The ground is no longer visible.
This flight among celestial bodies is critical.
Eternal ceilings, supernatural floors
therein lies potential,
limited not to the skies.
Our lives are magnified Petri dishes,
so we imagine more than we can attain
and hope it rings true like silent birthday wishes.
Unearth the strength to sustain.
Stars whisper prophetic words,
esoteric revelations.
My purpose made clear through these consultations.
My belief grounded as featherless birds.
Yet for every dream there's a nightmare,
like a comet slicing through the night air.
A morning of joy for every slight scare.

Prodigal Son

My emotional gravity,
keeping me grounded in spite of.
Though I fight love, it lives here.
A maelstrom of feelings,
nostalgic anxiety,
relief's way of healing.
A passage through gates,
I thought I'd have to die to see.
Hate to witness your beauty yielding.
Gone is the steel, replaced by abandoned buildings,
stained with hard times, solemn chimes.
The lights atop north side irradiates
the darkness, internecine clout,
guidance we can't live without,
beacon of hope

They say you've lost your luster
I say you just evolved.
What's more to be gained,
when you gave all you could muster?
Impermeable resolve remained.
To the trains passing through west side,
a nuisance turned token for a free ride.
Let our staple of memories;
be built not on my absence or sympathy,
but on a bond of cohesion,
present with me.
I bid you farewell

Black Mannequin

We survived a haunting past,
a daunting task, to say the least.
To bare a scar dark as molasses,
for all to see.
Yet justice still wears tinted glasses.
Torment and ridicule,
ornaments on a tree of hatred,
circumvents the roots of love,
all else is minuscule.
Our greatest fear isn't what we're scared of,
it's what we refuse to accept,
the power we choose to neglect.
Wisdom or serendipity,
a mix of synchronicity and fate.
I tried to masquerade in success, but what it hides,
it reveals in duress.
Still, I'm penned in
between the machine and forefather's strides.
I tried to bite my tongue,
to avoid the branches
where segregation hung.
Tried to blend in,
where dividing lines hinge.
That day I felt my pride cringe.
Even when you're indifferent,
the world will always see a skin pigment.

Soul Searching

Memories glowing,
gliding, flying,
with the zeal of a freed phoenix.
A thirst for success,
still chained superfluous.
If I had a hunger,
for virtuosity,
and chased it with the same vigor,
would I need that key?
Is it normal to be lost routinely?
To be a maverick to the world's stable?
To imagine comfort in dejected?
To provoke change until
its answer suffices?
Whistling winds of perplexity.
With trembling outstretched hands,
I snatch the lust of admiration.
A spirit masked by
wicked intentions,
the lap belt around
my guilty conscience.
A recurrent, twisting
merry-go-round.
But every sinner has a future.
Does my present,
resemble every saints past?
Arduous pursuit of serenity,
a soul's entity of solace.
I must find my purpose,
orbiting the realm
of consciousness,
and maintain it
with the stamina of nature.
My secret lifetime love affair.

When Death Knocks

Legacies we leave,
melancholy for the bereaved.
Tangled webs woven and forgiven,
new ones are weaved.
The last grains of sand,
funnel through our hour glass.
That dark tunnel we must pass,
peasants to God's command.
The inner voice that advises and curtails.
Wind shifting between the cattails
on the prairie, sights we rarely
get to appreciate before it's too late.
When death knocks for me,
cry not, but live like
it may ask for you tomorrow.

Dear God

Kneeling at your throne,
to worship, forever and a day.
For your grace is just a stone's throw away,
though our heart is error prone,
we're never alone.
Your spirit, angelic chaperon,
yet we wander from your instruction,
pilots of our won destruction.
Gripping the trigger of greed,
adopting the offspring violence breeds,
we're beckoned by poverty,
who multiplies before she feeds.
There's no novelty under the sun.
When righteousness is forthcoming,
we'd rather dance with our shortcomings,
find shade in our limitations.
Grant us divine inspiration,
we're knowingly incomplete within.
Craving worldly scented sin,
condemned by our indulgence,
Reborn from the cloth your son stemmed.
If you could remold the clay,
would we still roam
on this sphere we call home?
Do you silently curse when we go astray?
Do you simply ask yourself why?
Diluted faith, please believe we try.
Our efforts are polluted in habits
we can't seem to break,
heartache that begets more heartache.
I vowed, if we could do it again,
we'd try to make you proud.

Elephant in the Room

Circus of procrastination,
the lull of deliberation,
void of discourse,
ivory wrapped remorse.
Brute-like constriction,
the ghosts who employed it.
Attempts at eviction
hastily avoided.
A simple idiom, applicable to lives,
sharpness of the misery comparable to knives.
Awkwardness second only to the elongated reticence.
An obvious elephant, matched in weight by its relevance.
Hindsight paints a picture of beautiful elegance.
Stubbornness perpetuates a gap once closed.
Deep seeded emotions give root to a tree exposed.
Forced to burden the weight of silence and be a victim of my restraint,
loved and lost without complaint.
Can't understand how one proposed solution makes two wrong.
Time heals all wounds but sometimes time takes too long.
Blossoming flowers in the spring, moments before they bloom,
refusing to be naive about this presence in the room.

Growing Pains

I muse manhood, decisions made
in the rapture of reflection,
where I'm my shadows shade.
With imperial views
come new perspectives,
attention to perception.
I took cues from my elders
who stressed mature objectives.
I must stand,
even when nothing goes as planned.
Fleet is karma's punches . . .
I smile as the snow crunches
beneath my feet.
I'm starting to grasp it,
though I've got a lot to learn.

Alter Ego

I want to save the world
but I doubt it'd return the favor.
There, morality whirled
to the sea of a sirens quaver.
Hence heroism is cast
into a hungry flame,
one in which the ego heats.
Its reign is far and vast.
I'd like to appreciate
beauty's every thread . . .
Lust is the monster under my bed
clutching at the sheets.
Even with the night light
it's hard to anticipate
when it'll poke its head,
God renew my sight.
I want to be lost in my escape,
but every liberty has a cost.
I want to have a heart of gold,
but it's only as strong as the demand.
I'd like to be bolder,
but life doesn't always go as planned.
I could be more humble and kind
but I have to make room for vanity.
I'd like to be considered a great mind,
but I fear losing my sanity.
Truthful or blunt
All that I can't have is what I really want.
However for my sake
that wish needs not come true.
Part of me wants the cake,
the other wants to eat it too

Bargain for Sanity

Just relax, make yourself
comfortable. I want you to
close your eyes, open
your ears and unlock your mind.
Picture yourself completely submerged
in a river, thoroughly rinsing
everything you've known.
There's no current pulling you
but the water is freezing.
Your thoughts are racing
and with each passing second
they gain downhill momentum.
Finally you decide enough is enough
and arise out of the water.
You stop at the foot of a forest,
full of exotic plants. The scent of
magnolias, mixed with a glow of
dandelions subdues your progress.
Luscious fruits seduce your peripherals.
As you continue on the path, come
across three enormous, freshly dug
graves. Upon closer inspection,
you can see the names on the headstones;
Racism, Hate, and War.
You close your eyes tightly then reopen them,
it reads the same. Now you're wondering
if this world exists, if it's real. Can we
have a world where war doesn't
bend the knuckles of peace?
Oh but we can . . . Look again

City of Hope

Collapsed patience, seen before confessed,
expressed but never mouthed,
this is the weight of the oppressed.
Whispers of the Campbell soup brand,
attracting tourists to see how
tall you used to stand,
and the cane aiding you now.
Your children laugh to keep from crying
but you're still fighting, trying.
Like you, I've had years where
I squeezed my eyelids to wish the bad away,
refusing to stare at what I became,
but that ends now, it ends today.
I see promise clotting the desolation.
I see hope overpowering desperation.
A rebirth herein.
You will kindle excitement again.
And though legislation has forgotten
about you, I haven't.
Be strong Camden

Antarctica

A magnet for solitude,
I need it more than
it needs me.
My hands dried from
the damp recollections
of yesteryear, of failed
attempts, my intuition
in contempt. My wardrobe
of happiness, bleached with
disappointments.
Retreating back to
my frozen safe haven,
greeted with a mythical chill.
I apologize with every return
and include a promise to learn,
a vow not to forget the
frigid home that raised me.
Peaceful and undisturbed
misconceived and quiet,
natures arms give me shelter.
One that I took for granted,
forgive me I was wrong.
Buried in deep thoughts,
rushed by time to make it right.
I'll climb rugged mountains,
swim raging seas if it'll
make things better. If it will
extinguish every distraction
before me, I'll walk one hundred
miles through the ice to find you.
You showed me the bright side
of bleak, healing beyond the breaking point.
You let me see the iceberg . . .
from beneath the surface.

Throne Without an Heir

Midnight oil burned,
stars cried, destiny spurned,
discipline rightfully earned,
from the past we learned.

The thunder's roar,
the grin that lightening wore,
in life's revolving door,
God's kept in the bottom drawer.

The sun, enchantment conversed,
the clouds dispersed,
fortunes reversed,
as if rehearsed,
the day grew fair,
as learned to care,
with love to spare.
Evil became a throne without an heir.

ACT II

Balloons in the attic

Trail Of Burning Roses

A mid-November chill
forebodes us from wearing hearts on our sleeves.
Forced to conceal
until we finally fall like multicolored leaves.
Timely resurrections,
vivid yet poignant recollections.
Take a leap of faith,
live with the consequence,
seeds of love in provenance.
Glimpses of adoration
turn to pleas for restoration.
Tragedies that patience scorns
long before the door closes,
igniting a trail of burning roses,
scorching thorns . .
When to a man's core, less than intuition,
beneath wishing.
To hover and not deplore,
swallowing loves closing without implore.
Gathering the strength to carry on
thus more, the urge to trust again.

Enchanted

Interlocked fingers
proclaiming a union
stronger than err before.
Feathery kisses,
delicate romance.
Our bodies intertwined
in the bliss of intimacy.
Gone were worries,
nothing else mattered.
Silent and tranquil
in each other's arms

Eternal window pane,
mirages of the moment.
Visions of timeless,
swiftly interrupted.
Ever so mindful,
the magic wand
of circumstance,
and its stoic nature

Naked trees
reaching for warmth,
majestic shadows, silhouettes.
Irresolute gestures,
obnoxious regrets.
Subtle creases before the fold.
Our memories bathe
in salty water
like ashes poured in the sea.

Unbreakable Heart

Liquid emotions soften
the carpet beneath me.
Sobs of hurt rang out
from an extinguished fire.
A pendulum of blame,
tossed back and forth.
The rush once felt
by her company
is poison in her absence.
Coveted one moment,
ceded the next.
"I love you" to
"why'd we rush?"
Scattered explanations.
If only time's hands
were double jointed.
Critical periods of mourning
that lead to a breakthrough.
Inside of every nerve,
every vessel, hope springs aloft

Sky Is Falling

The ground quivered when I released my shield.
My surrender, sorrowfully trite.
I remember losing without a fight,
vulnerability promptly peeled.
Trust, the colt driving our chariot dissolved.
Soon-to-be came to a screeching halt,
a bridge bluffed, not endeavored.
Chemistry slowly gained, quickly severed.
Hollow promises of forever
that we'll never see.
40 days, 39 1/2 nights we were teased,
pleased, for all that pleasing is worth.
Eased into a paralyzing comfort.
Our words became swords, fencing
in the spirit of distrust, wincing
at every cut. Intents to maim.
My head hung lower than shame,
I'm remiss when love's at stake.
Yet I wonder, when I'm lying awake,
peering, as if finding you through the abyss,
are you doing the same?

Fallen Temple

The temple was built, I watched it fall.
Little by little, it crumbled.
Arguments born in rage
would lead to degrees of separation,
with it, orders to pack.
We packed hearty and never
questioned why or what for.
Then we'd leave,
with troubled minds,
toting bloated suitcases.

The temple was built, I watched it fall.
It buckled for years;
they struggled,
stringing each other's nerves
until resilience receded.
Unresolved conflicts
reared to strain their union.
Heat-of-the moment screams,
chased with awkward silences
and apologetic pleas.
Parental responsibilities
had resolve postponed.

The temple was built, I watched it fall.
The dust rose with its collapse.
Ornery spirits punctuated
a disharmony that could
be deemed unsuitable.
Disgusted glances
at a picture once painted beautiful.

Nightingale

Admitted to an anguish
of which I never enrolled,
driven by anxious machines
I thought I controlled.
Remedies discontent
with repairing, where art thou nightingale?

I've hurled my ego,
rebelling from the world.
Stripped by its bitterness,
clothed by the wilderness.
Fragranced by fears,
crying invisible tears
like a frightened whale,
comfort me nightingale.

Curiosity is pivotal
among faded dreams growing pitiful.
I'm crawling to my pinnacle,
every inch, every syllable.
Overwhelmed by morning ails,
sing to me nightingale.

Words for Tears

The words that go with these tears,
originate from a place dimly lit and tucked away.
From an address where love once resided.
From shouts harshly spoken,
unable to be refunded.
From obstacles and tribulations
that have defined me,
but slowly they chip away
at the foundation of my being.
From tombstones that were once loved ones,
who've seen my God above,
but can't feel my love from below.
From avenues of hurt,
splints of broken promises.
From deep fears and deeper remorse.
From apologies that cover half the damage they caused.
They come behind eyelids for a dam,
buckling under the pressure.

ACT III
Strides of angels

Until We Meet Again

Passing often grants us mixed feelings.
An ascension to heaven, yet we're left reeling,
silent in disbelief.
A soul's destination met with relief.
It says something about a man
when you die and it benefits God's plan.
One's loss is another's gain;
let his passion stain our memory . . .
Very shocked when I heard the news,
part of me was still sitting in the pews.
I figure angels must be in short supply,
cause friends and loved ones shouldn't have to say goodbye.
Hard to console the hearts that grieve after the pain,
easy to forget sometimes that a rainbow comes after the rain.
He gave us lessons of wisdom to follow
and no matter how optimistic, this is a tough pill to swallow.
God engineered a path for the souls of living water, and Doug was the light.
So the comfort that comes to us now is knowing that he is alright.
He put a smile on every person he met,
all the jokes, the laughs, and the stories we won't soon forget.
Even though the night carries weeping and mourning,
rest assured joy shall see you in the morning . . .
So . . . In honor of a life well lived, not by the number of years
but the way he lived them, let not your remorse
be remembered by the number of tears,
but by the way you live your life from here on out.
Like you, my faith won't wither nor fade
I won't forget the promise I made to you Doug

To Pastor Doug Hogan and the Hogan family

9 years in December

The days have grown dull,
the pains often and sharp.
Distance has taken its toll.
A broken cadence, golden harp
of silence. Continuity gone,
even divided we're drawn.
We're family, spheres of support.
Though our vision's clear,
sometimes we lose sight of things,
puppets to the strings above us.
It hurts that lost time
struck without admonition.
One mountain's crucial climb
and a determined disposition.
Deep down, I know how you feel;
the gloom makes it hard to heal.
It seems wrong for parents to separate.
As you get older
the complexities will penetrate,
at that moment, I will be your shoulder.
I'm always thinking about you,
how much I've missed and how much you've grown too

Just A Wish

I wish God had let you stay.
My heart became a stray,
if home is where the heart is.
Sometimes death answers life's quiz.
Your presence, now irretrievable,
was simply unbelievable.
The pretty brown windows to your soul
rid me of chagrin.
I'd give my sight to see them again,
if we could have one more stroll.
Much like the truth is a sponge for lies,
your memory is tissue for teary eyes.

I wish God had let you stay,
it hurts to say goodbye this way.
Your spirit that never quit,
your grace, and your wit.
Your dark hair that flowed as the Amazon,
gone but not forgotten the antiphon.
Loss paves a road often rough, but if I look up high enough,
will I find you? Will I see you?
If I pray without ceasing, will I free you?
Would you willingly flee,
from a place you ought to be?
Ijustmissyou

Mama

The visibility is slow to improve
since pain's drapes are hard to remove.
Strong winds can make even sturdy trees sway.
It hurt every Mother's Day.
Twenty years of birthdays that you missed,
countless fists raised in anger,
before clutching the wrist of faith.
The guilt we cleansed each other of,
nothing like a mother's love.
I've cared,
even dared to confront the monster,
who split the infrastructure we once shared.
I don't blame you for the choice you made.
I blossomed from your support and aid,
paving a blue collar plan.
I've become a respectable young man,
finished school, found love and lost it too.
Pursuing dreams like you'd want me to.
Varnish, ameliorate the silver lining,
may it shine and never tarnish.
Channels of endless growth
through inhibition.
Time apart has burned us both
beyond recognition
but through my veins your blood flows,
God knows I'll find you one day

ACT IV
Joys painted marvelous

The Calm

An escape to a humble abode,
secret passage to a middle ground,
in the proverbial fork in the road.
The time is now, hope is found.
Moment for rejoice;
listen for a still voice
steady as sleep,
to visit as nevermore.
Questions to ask, answers to find
until it resonates deep
within the reservoirs
of one's mind.
Impetuous thoughts gagging
the gaiety from our rise,
bragging a formidable repugnance
and abundance of lost souls.
Iridescent skies,
windows to an omnipresent savior,
a sight to savor.
Wisdom spoken through psalms.
Ignoring the numbness in my palms,
climbing heavens ladder, reaching higher.

Life's a Marathon

In April, things will be different.
I will turn a new leaf,
and from the stem of understanding,
I'll find wisdom.
With a deep breath
I'll acknowledge
our child-like wonder,
replaced with constant fretting.
Our pace, growth
quickened by peer pressure
and society's measures.
Courage is the antidote
to these adversaries,
wear it as a badge of honor.

Crimson stained boots of war.
Fear hidden in camouflaged garments,
adversity is sweat on the brow of progress.
We march on, groaning,
wailing to the hills of Zion.
At times I'm just a tortoise
in life's race.
Armed with a hard shell
and a determination
to make it to the shore,
free from the snares of the world.
Above all else know that
on this ride, where speed is plentiful,
and brakes are few,
a crash is inevitable.
But rise out of the wreckage
a new man, a new woman.

Gate of Paradise

Time moves fast enough for the days to pass as hours.
Adrenaline consumes you till you can feel its power.
Your will . . . the main component,
the absolute moment of all moments.
Everything you've got, a simple vow to keep.
Failure is what you're redeemed of.
Capture the here and now or forever sleep,
for this is everything you've dreamed of.
Trial and error, once a teacher, now a principle,
carefully instructing the way of sensible.
All that you've gone through serves as preparation,
your drive breeds separation.
Pressure pulls you,
you're not moved by its pulling, it fuels you.
Tunnel vision to the gate of paradise.
The wait is over.

At Long Last

Feelings of every sort flash before my eyes,
images that we epitomize.
Tales of ageless love, now odd to see,
my heart rests on this odyssey.
Thou art equal to the sights of heaven above
and the wonders o f the world below.
Hence a longing I'll never outgrow.
A thirst quenched from a fountain drop.
Your radiance brings out the best in me
like sunlight overlooking the mountaintop.
Rest assured you can invest in me.
Hastened pulse and a prolonged grin,
chain reactions to a change within.
Your the temple where my faith dwells,
the reason my passion swells,
I'm drawn to you, if you couldn't tell.
Though you disguise it well,
I behold an angel!

Fathers Love

In some way we're inseparable,
through valleys of concealment,
where strained affinity was acceptable.
I found fulfillment
in a sky of lonesome, where stars
were few and far.

I never meant to eradicate
a family you helped fabricate.
We were both stuck in our ways,
too stubborn to change.
The pains of an adolescent phase,
it was strange, we wanted more,
but we settled for less.

On the fingertip of a breakthrough,
I'd find a hiatus to escape to,
darting to the extremities of sadness.
There was a method to your madness.
We never hid our imperfections,
so in the mirror we stared,
true feelings were bared,
till we couldn't stand our reflections.
I played my hand of cards,
tip-toeing over broken shards of confusing.
Happiness was my allusion.
Above it all I learned
some battles aren't worth the fight,
two wrongs always oppose right,
experience means wisdom was earned.

During a bedside conversation,
I saw the wink of exultation,
I saw time heal,
and completely fill wounds inches deep,
saw a second chance to repair,
wrongdoings, a breath of fresh air.
This cancer that has you inflicted
shall not last,
this will also pass.
Prayers I pray until you're lifted.
Our road to redemption will carry on
over a new found exemption.
I love you, sorry it took so long

Exoneration

To flee is life, living freely,
fleeing all that troubles me.
My vase of resilience mended,
second wind for the winded.
Like misfortune wasn't banished,
just temporarily rescinded.
Pain vanished, my thoughts
cleansed in a stream of clarity,
to close the disparity
between the man I am,
and the one I could be.
This sacred pen bleeds purposely,
my sacrificial lamb.
Now capture what you deserve,
and at all costs, preserve
your sculpture of happiness

Beach Chair

Ecstasy, spirit of elation,
the light which follows privation,
visit me early and often.
Your highs soften my lows.
The face beneath your disguise unveils
greener pastures and bluer skies
that fuel a euphoric rise
far beyond what the eyes can see.
The tight embrace of triumph,
hard to forfeit.
Sincere delight I can't replace.
It's easy to forget the simple joys that make us smile,
that make us cry, and sigh all the while.
Guard your plans from the sinking sand,
and surf the wave of life
the best you can.

100 Hills

Motionless meditation,
oasis of openness
to counter my cubicle of recluse.
Idealist for peace I can't produce.
I'm a visionary in these distant plains,
mundane and ordinary.
Hallowed ground, diminished stains.
Journey on a hundred hills,
thriving off fatigue, throbbing thrills,
to free prodigious knowledge instilled.
Too prideful to see,
actions tooled and chiseled worthless,
once blind to the waking dreams of purpose.
Lost in the rigors of the day
is the stillness of the night,
the glimmer of the moon, the plight of prayers,
when the clouds float away.

Nirvana

Women of the earth,
wonders of the world.
Magnificent creatures,
precious beyond compare.
Your strength, found
not in physical prowess,
but in capabilities
unknown to man.
Just as you bring forth life,
you bring meaning to life.
I say to those who've been mistreated,
hurt, unappreciated,
deceived, misunderstood,
abused, manipulated . . .
Lost lies within an
arm's reach of being found.
Inside the secret door
behind the wall you've been
building for years, there's a place
brimming with love.
Let us escape to that place,
where your worth is recognized.
A place that reverberates
the voice inside you pleading,
screaming "You deserve more!!"

Insuperable Summer

To have you on a string,
to pull you close,
the difference it would bring,
to have you near,
at a moment's notice.
Pardon my selfishness,
I'll share when satisfaction fills me.
Nine months is far
too long to wait.
Even patience would
tap its fingers.
Unlike yourself,
my youthfulness
will fade over time.
What happens then?
Will I be replaced,
forced to swallow acceptance?
My love for you
rises with a sun
that never sets.
Remember how we met?
The flowers I bought,
how we spoke without sound.
Then with your hand in mine
we danced without music.
Just subtle movements,
that mimicked undying felicity,
carved in memory.

The Calling

Seeds planted with
divine hands, void
of gambled fates.
A fire lit on
our heart's mantle.
The secret we yearn
to know. In due season
it is revealed.
We're made whole
by the revelation,
made complete.
The common breeze
that awakens our
senses, gives new life.
The sky, a perceived
limit, now substitutes
as a launching pad.
A select few are chosen
out of the many called.
How a pen can bring calm,
its ink, dopamine.
Stretching the mind's
appendages. This
is my spaceship to the
gravity of stress, my
acceptance to the wink
of misfortune. I write to free
my soul. Perhaps through its
freedom, yours will never be bound.

Garden of Olives

Ambiguous relations
blessed with second chances,
cursed in accidents of timing.
Meetings through happenstance,
prayers molded real.
When that fairytale
unfolded before me,
I remember smiling
as wide as dew
glistening over blades of grass.
I sat still, but my heart
paced back and forth.
390 miles occupies the archway
dividing daydreams from reality.
The vital yet overlooked gap
between confused and happy,
between love and sane.
If I could've spoken
I would've said
thank you! I would've
asked if I'd ever see
you again.
I was on cloud nine,
seeking the one after.
Like for one night
I could bare my soul,
pour out my heart
and not fear. I could live
and not worry death.

I'm made less by the
feelings you gave, made
shallow by your depth,
made translucent by your smile.
Your laugh gave me courage.
If I could make joy
your average day.
I could spend a lifetime
proving the validity behind
these feelings. Love at
first sight, a stretch few
can reach. Some hearts are
made more elastic than others.

Leaking Pen

My addiction and my cure,
my unconditional love.
This pen, the couch
I lie on before rattling
off all my problems.
The long awaited answer
when it feels I'm asking in vain.
It's my hand stitched
quilt of dreams,
whose abilities never
pale in comparison.
It's the tape recorder
for my mind's voice,
my stilts when I'm belittled.
My feeling in a world
numb with cold,
emptying my heart of fear,
my mind of distress.
All that remains are
portraits painted by
loud colors and soft words.
Spoken in such a way,
its image cannot fade.

Aphrodite

Hail to a Goddess
whose truth fails to be modest.
Our souls are braille for her blindness.
She can give a high unlike any drug.
I dug deep to make room for her presence . .
In return she gave me a glimpse
of a force where glee flies and sorrow limps.
Pure motives isn't asking for much,
how we long for human touch,
nourished from the bosom of passion.
Without it we're vessels painted ashen.
Each equal to the sum of parts, let her
sip from the springs of honest hearts.
Our trust and devotion,
joined at the seat of affection,
moments made intimate by their connection.
Much more than an emotion.
Alas, when you've tight roped the mountain side
with closed eyes, carrying only a wide grin,
anticipating who's on the other side.
You'll find her, exult then,
but you must not let her go.

The Town

Memories jolted to the forefront,
august in texture,
vibrant in nature.
Some are pacified,
staring behind
the bars of reality.
I beg to differ,
releasing my cares
inside this superlative view.
My private flight of stairs,
spiraling above the earth.
Strongly compelled,
I gravitate to
the summit of a hill,
overlooking a small town.
Quiet and peace make
way for me.
The air is a mixture
of fresh and free.
Here, the light and dark
contrast ensnares
the attentive eye.
The lights gleam the town
wondrously, making every
night seem like a holiday.

Bittersweet Rainbow

At first glance,
today may be unlucky.
With the fog filled air
and the sun drowned in the doldrums.
Even the birds chirp cautiously.
I stare out across
emptiness, reflectively.

Reaching my hand out,
I can feel the rain
coming down gently.
Today's doom is all but secured.
The chirp simmers
down to a whisper.
I'm reminded of voices
I can still hear,
living or not,
that sound just a shoulder tap
away. On these gloomy
days they are clearer,
and no matter the case,
messages of caution
and wisdom are constant.
At second glance,
the clouds slowly began to part;
the day may be fair after all.
Anxiety follows me,
we brace for the glow
of the hottest star.
For its arrival will bring
forth a rainbow.

Tranquility Retrieves Understanding Everyday/ T.R.U.E.

The creases our
tears trace also
construct wonderful smiles.
The simplest things
that bring joy to others.
Unity grew to peacefulness,
like a lullaby before the dream.
Mighty will before
imposing immorality.
David's before Goliath's
of the latter.
Progression, held refuge
behind a glass shelter
that will surely crack
before it shatters.
Simplify the reasons
difficult to fathom.
Look forward not back,
by no means down, always up.
We must persevere,
our hope shines through fear;
light in the darkness.
Off branches of doubt
we'll leap into a strong draft,
catapulting us skyward.
I tell you, we're almost, we're almost there!

ACT V

Receipts of homage

© 2011 Adam Romanowicz - 3scape.com

'Where I'm From'

I'm from the hill,
a small village in the middle of nowhere.
From preparation for the real world.
I'm from the broken down wheel burrow
with the flat tire,
loading wood in the winter time.
Brushing my hands together over the warm fire.
To soft spoken but hard headed.
I'm from pass-me-down clothes
and eight dollar shoes.
From wise uncles and noisy neighbors,
whoopings on the hind pots till I couldn't sit.
I'm from summers in the country,
tick bites and no cable.
From the napkin, damp with saliva,
to clean my face.
Dusting off trophy cases,
looking back on younger stage glories.
I'm from 'when I was your age' stories.
From asphalt races, to riding down
danger hill at break-neck speed.
From countless trips to Getty's,
to spend money I didn't have.
From funny ain't a sense of humor,
it's a lifestyle.
To climbing trees and playing ball till night fall,
I'm from dreams of wishing to be tall.
From clip-on ties and Sunday school,
fancy china dishes after service.
To being a reluctant but avid class clown.
I'm from the careful eye of Mrs. Rose.
From punishment without pity,
from lit up to let down,
I am from those moments.
A leaf coerced by its design,
displaying illimitable worth
deeply rooted in the family tree

59

Ode to Keats

When fears arise that I may cease to be
before my potential has reached its heights,
before I've truly found my purpose here,
before threescore and ten.
When I observe, upon the sky's surface,
rays of peace and riddles of love lost,
and I think that I may expire before
I interpret them,
with the scent of opportunity
and when I feel, magnificent wonder,
that I shall never capture thee again,
never utter your name,
or speak of un-mercurial love . .
I sit forsaken at the doorstep
of an unforgiving world

Ode to Kipling

If you can face all of your failures
and not let them consume you,
but be motivated by their existence.
If you can paint examples of faithfulness
from your actions, not your words.
If you can see a plan from end to beginning,
and never lose the vision.
If you can bear to see a blessing
you longed to have, short lived,
and still live blameless.
If you can carry your family through
tribulation and say nothing of its weight.
If you can admit your wrongs,
no matter the crime.
And make mistakes,, only one time each.
If you can lend a helping hand and ask
for nothing in return.
If you can be a pillar of strength,
when scared yourself.
Or detach from excuses, regardless
of the consequences the world will be yours,
as a bonus you'll be a man too